A
FATHERLESS
DAUGHTER

Annette Elliott Douglas

ISBN: 978-1-7337610-8-6

Disclaimer

This book is designed to share the author's life experiences and revelations. The author does not claim that the experiences and decisions shared within the book are ones the reader will experience or have experienced. The information shared within this book highlights a few difficulties and drawbacks that the author experienced and how she overcame them. Sound efforts have been made for content accuracy. This book has not been written to condemn, point fingers, or target anyone. As a result, you agree never to sue or hold the author liable for any claims or similarities arising from the information contained within this book. Any likenesses to actual persons, alive or deceased, or personal experiences are merely to share the journey through the author's eyes. You agree to be bound by this disclaimer.

Dedication

This book is dedicated to my parents, Bernice Elliott-Lockhart & Daniel William Elliott, and my grandparents, James & Irene Brown. May God bless your souls. To my bonus dad, Hubert Lockhart, and my 1st true loves, my daughters Ronisha & Ikesha - thank you for helping me to understand the true meaning of unconditional love. To my bonus children, Gerric, Jamell & Kaela, and all 12 of my grands, along with my two great-grands, I love you guys to the moon and back. Finally, to my husband, Eric L. Douglas, the love of my life, my encourager, my support system, and my #1 fan - thank you (He) for letting me be me (She), and yet you still love me.

Annette Elliott Douglas

WHAT'S INSIDE

Acknowledgments

First and foremost, I would like to thank God for his never-ending grace, mercy, and love during the preparation of this book. Second, I want to thank my mother, Bernice, for sharing these stories (with me) about my father, which inspired me to write this book. Although, she's no longer here to witness my extraordinary accomplishment. I know she's looking down on me from Heaven with a big smile.

To my loving and patient husband, Eric, for always supporting me in whatever I do and being my sounding board. To my daughter Ronisha for being that listening ear and helping design my book cover. To my daughter Ikesha for always encouraging me to keep going.

To my Starlights, Ma. Margaret, Auntie Cora, My sisters Rachell, Connie, Henrietta, & Kim. Thank you for all the memories we created from Florida to Georgia and all in between. There will never be another chicken shack (LOL).

To my brothers, Eddie, Charles, and Greg, for always being there whenever I needed you.

Thanks to ALL my family and friends who have supported me throughout the years and to my three very special friends, Kesia, Serena, and Debra, for all the tears, laughs, and hours of conversations we have shared.

Foreword

A Fatherless Daughter allows one to embark upon a journey from a young girl's lifeless and hopeless beginning to a grown-up, victorious, happily ever after, all without a biological father. With the help of God, family, and friends, she is an overcomer and living her best life. This memoir I speak of is not a fairy tale; but of miracles, signs, and wonders experienced by the author of this book, my forever friend of 24 years, Annette Elliott Douglas.

It is said that the absence of a father creates trauma that necessitates healing. It hurts if you know your father is absent but imagine if the conscious knows you will never (ever) see or know him. The staining residue that remains conveys emotional damage and deceitful thoughts of untruths about who you are, conspired by the enemy's tactics. At some point in this life, many daughters will choose a mate unsuitable for them due to a longing for love or a lack of guidance or experience from a father.

Despite the challenges that lie ahead, there was always something special about Annette. Everyone around her loves her. She has a gentle smile and a caring nature and holds true to what or to whomever she has committed. She does not allow her unfortunate circumstance to dictate her future. Life is good.

The most vital parts of developing into the noblewoman she stands for are: 1) her intentionality when loving and caring for others; 2) the deepening of her knowledge of her father in heaven; 3) her relationship with her father in heaven. God's word from Psalm 32:8 states I will instruct you and teach you in the way you should go: I will counsel you with my eye upon you, and she believed it. It is in her faith that she finds that God is a healer and a provider.

A Fatherless Daughter will be a blessing to anyone who dares to believe that God is a father to the fatherless, and he is more than enough. Through this book, a father may be enticed to enhance his relationships by realizing how great of a role he plays in one's life. A daughter can find her knight in shining armor, or should I say, her Boaz. Hope is not lost. It can be found in Jesus.

Day by day, as you connect with God, reflect and visualize the words written in this book. You, you, and you can experience what we call the 3 R's - Renewal, Revelation, and Restoration.

Thank you, Annette, for allowing me to be a part of your journey. I have learned truth, love, family, and friendship through your life. Forever grateful.

Dakesia Collins Campbell

Introduction

Have you ever asked yourself, "Why do I do the things that I do? Or what affects my decision-making? Do you ever feel that you are all alone, even when you are in a room full of people? Do you ever wonder if you will ever be happy? If you answered "yes" to any of these questions, you chose the right book to read.

I invite you to take a short journey with me as I walk through parts of my life. Believe it or not, I have asked myself those same questions. A Fatherless Daughter may not be for everyone, but if you have ever felt lost, this book may help shine a light on what you think is a dark time. This book will not solve your problems, but it will take your mind off them for a little while. Who knows. During your reading, there may be a spark in you to do something different in your life.

I pray that you are inspired, encouraged, enlightened, and, most of all, that you gain a more intimate relationship with God. **Renew, Refocus, Release, Revive, and Live**.

Young Love

The little that I know about my father, as told to me by my mother, was that he was a very handsome young man. He stood about 6 feet tall, with pecan brown skin, sexy dark brown eyes, and natural black curly hair. He was a very stylish dresser, displayed by the nice suits that he would wear. Allow me to paint the scene. My father lived during the early fifties and sixties when it was customary for young black men to wear suits, and my father was no exception. He would step out in his single-breasted, two-buttons-down-the-front suit in a dark color with a plain textured skinny tie, white dress shirt, a handkerchief folded and neatly placed in his breast pocket, and sometimes with a tie clip. Let's not forget the fashion-forward and highly polished black shoes. He would top his outfit off with a nice felt fedora. Simply put, the brother was always clean. "Clean as the board of health," my grandmother would say. He had suits in all colors grey, black, brown, white, and tan, with everything, always matching, including the fedoras.

A Fatherless Daughter

He caught my mother's eye with his debonairness. She was trying to play hard to get but little did she know she had caught his eye too. He told his friends, "She's going to be my wife one day," not knowing how true that statement was. They both were sixteen when they met and began to date secretly. My mother often asked my grandmother if she and her little sister, Sandra, could see a movie. The movie request was a ploy to sneak and see my father.

After about a year of secretly dating, they decided they could not live without each other. Thus, a decision was made to take it to the next level. So, the lovebirds made a pack that when they (both) turned eighteen, they would get married. Guess what? My mother turned eighteen on October 2, 1960, and my father turned eighteen on February 21, 1961. So, in keeping with their decision, wedding plans began, and marriage is precisely what they did.

My grandmother was living in Florida at the time. She traveled to New York to help with the wedding plans. My parents were married in June of 1961. I am unsure of the actual day. *Did I mention my mother was three months pregnant with me when they were married*? No? Well, she was. Stay tuned to discover more about my entrance into this world.

Their wedding day was one of the happiest days of my parent's life. They were finally married, and according to my mother, she had married the love of her life. She was so in love with my father, and my father was so in love with her. The wedding went on with only one hiccup. The photographer took plenty of pictures, but unfortunately, he had not taken the lens cover off the camera. As a result, none of the images were visible or could be printed. So, you have to ask yourself, what was God up to?

Thus, on this picture-perfect day, no memories were captured on camera. However, I was able to see one picture of my parents on their wedding day. This picture was taken outside my father's parent's house, Nana & Big Danny. However, the images were so far away that they looked like cake toppers on a wedding cake. It turns out that that would be the only picture I would see with my father in it, and *I could not even see his face*.

Turn of Events

Have you ever experienced or heard a story that alters the direction of the people's lives in the story? My mother shared a story that portrayed a turn of events that no one would want or expect to experience.

Approximately one week after she and my father married, they moved into a fully furnished studio apartment in Jamaica Queens, New York. One evening when they had gone to bed. Once in bed, they began talking as they often did, and out of the blue, my father asked her if she believed in ghosts. Of course, this had to have surprised her, so she asked, "why?" He said, "well, if I die before you, I will come back to you, not to scare you, but just to let you know that I love you, and you will know that it is me." She looked at him with a bizarre look, as one can only imagine, and said, "well, ok, if you say so, but we won't have to worry about that for a while." Little did she know it would be sooner than she would have ever imagined.

Young Love

Exactly two weeks after this conversation, on July 27, 1961, my father got up to get ready for work as he had done in the previous weeks. He ate breakfast, kissed my mother goodbye, and said he would see her later. Then, he headed off to work. My mother did not know that it would be her last kiss from my father. She had no idea it would be the last time she would see her husband, best friend, or her baby's father alive.

The day went on as usual. 5:00 pm was approaching, when my father would typically return home from work. As my mother prepared dinner, she looked up at the clock and noticed that it was 5:30 pm and no Danny was in sight. After about two hours of waiting and still no Danny in sight, my mother went to my grandparent's house to see if he had stopped there before coming home. Once she arrived, she asked my grandparents if he was there. Their response was no and that they had not seen him. They told her to go back home and not to worry. He should be home soon. They thought he might have stopped at a friend's house before coming home.

So, my mom went back home and waited, and waited, and waited. It was getting close to midnight, and Danny still had not called or come home. She called the friends she knew of, but none of them had seen or heard from him. Her emotions went from being angry to scared to worried. She had felt that she had waited long enough. Finally, she decided to call the police department to file a missing person report. They told her they could do nothing because she had to wait 24 hours before filing a missing person report.

The following day, she woke up with no Danny in the bed or the apartment. She then called the police department for the second time to file the missing person report. During this call, she was advised that they did have a "John Doe" in the county morgue, and if she wanted to come to make an identification, she could do so. My mother called my grandparents and told them my father did not come home. She expressed that it was not my father's character and that something was wrong. She shared with my grandparents that she had called the police department twice. The first time, they told her that she had to wait 24 hours to file a missing person report. The second time, they stated that they had a "John Doe" at the county morgue, and she could come to make an identification. So, my mom and grandparents headed to the county morgue, about 30 minutes away. The drive must have been the longest 30 minutes of my mother's life. She sat in the back seat, looking out the window. There was nothing she could do but stare out the window watching cars, big trees, people sitting at the bus stops, and kids playing in the streets after opening the fire hydrant with water spraying everywhere as they drove to the morgue. All kinds of thoughts were going through her head. "Please don't let it be my husband. He was supposed to be at work. What has happened to him? I pray he's alright." Then, the sound of "Bernice, Bernice, Bernice" woke her from her trance. They had finally arrived at the county morgue.

They walked into the morgue and approached the receptionist's desk. They asked the receptionist if they were in the right place to make possible identification of a "John Doe" that was brought in some time yesterday. The receptionist asked for their names and then asked them to have a seat. She stated that someone would come to retrieve them shortly. The waiting game was on again, and another ten minutes seemed like an eternity.

A lady dressed in blue scrubs (finally) approached and said, "Mr. Elliott?" They all stood up. The lady in the blue scrubs said, "follow me." They walked down a hallway, passing room after room after room. Finally, when they reached the elevator, they all entered. The lady pressed the "B" button on the panel board. The elevator doors closed, and after about 20 seconds, the doors opened. They all exited the elevator and walked down a hallway. Once at the end of the hallway, they made a right turn. Suddenly, they were facing a door that read County Morgue.

My mother could not take another step. So, she and my grandmother stayed in the hallway while my grandfather entered the room to identify the "John Doe." Meanwhile, my mom began to pray that the person inside was not the love of her life lying in that cold morgue. Another waiting game began. Finally, my grandfather came out with his head held down, tears streaming down his face, and his eyes were red as fire. He could hardly speak, but he mustered up enough energy to say, "Yes, it's Danny." My mother said it felt like someone had stabbed her in her heart, turned the knife, and pulled her heart out. She was in disbelief. How could this be? It must be a dream. Please wake me up, she thought. She and my grandmother just embraced each other with tears flowing like a river. My mother was so weak that she could hardly walk. Therefore, they sat her in a chair right there in the hallway. It was not a dream.

My father had been found on a park bench after being beaten to death. His wallet was stolen, which explains why he did not have any identification. After beating him, they placed a newspaper over his face as his body slumped over on the bench. Now would be a good time to share that my father was part of a gang. However, he wanted out when he decided to get married and start a family. I guess once you are in, there is no way out other than by death. Was this a gang-related murder? Could it have been a robbery gone wrong? Well, I guess we will never know. It was just another young black man's death during that era. In the eyes of the law, "oh well, life goes on."

For my mother, Danny's sudden departure was not that easy. At that moment, her life changed forever. In December of that same year, 1961, a beautiful baby girl was born, and she was named Annette Elease Elliott.

The Visitation

The visitation was one of the many stories shared with me by my mother. Another memorable story involved visiting my grandmother's sister, Aunt Clara, who lived in Philadelphia. At the time, I was approximately five years old. The trip began with a train ride from Grand Central Station to Philadelphia. As we headed to the track to catch our train, suddenly, the crowd seemed to separate. A man was walking towards us down the middle of the divided crowd. My mom squeezed my hand tight and said, "Oh my God." The man approaching us looked exactly like my father. The closer he got, the harder she squeezed my hand. As he came near us and they passed each other, she was afraid to look at him. She was even more afraid to turn around and look back at him. Finally, however, she turned to look at him. The man had his left hand behind his back, so she could see his wedding band, which matched hers. She then looked down at me for a split second in disbelief. When she turned to look at the man again, he was gone.

At that moment, she was freaking out. Why? She recalled the conversation she and my father had two weeks after marriage. He told her that he would come to her and that she would know that it was him. Things that make you go, hmmm, right?

"Let him kiss me with the kisses of his mouth - for your love is more delightful than wine."

Song of Songs 1:2 ~ New International Version

The Great Debut

Annette Elease Elliott made her great debut on Tuesday, December 19, 1961, weighing in at a whopping 6 lbs and 5 oz in the basement of Morton Plant Hospital in Clearwater, FL. I was born in the deep south, when everything was still segregated. Hence, the reason that I was in the basement of the hospital. Two years later, in 1963, my family moved back to New York, the state where it all started, where the seed of my father was planted, and I was conceived.

My mother and I lived with my grandparents, James & Irene Brown. I thank God for them both. We lived in a two-bedroom apartment in Cunningham Heights, Queens, New York. It was not until I was seven or eight that I could go outside and play with my friends. Cunningham Heights did not compare to the good outdoors down south in Florida, where I eventually began spending summers with my family and friends. In New York, I could only play immediately in front of our apartment building, where my mom could see me from the window. My friends and I enjoyed outdoor activities such as double-dutch jump rope, hopscotch, tag, and red-light-green light, to name a few.

Looking back, these were the good ole days when children enjoyed the outdoors, and you didn't worry about children being kidnapped. Yet, my mom would always tell me, "Annette, you can go outside and play, but do not you go inside anyone's home." I would reassure her by saying, "Okay, mommy, I won't." I cannot explain what happened to my brain cells. It must have been that New York air because as soon as I got outside, the entire conversation that my mom and I had would escape my memory bank. As soon as one of my friends mentioned, "I got barbies at my house. Do you want to go play with them?" My answer would be "yes," and off I would go. There is one day in particular that I recall vividly to this day. My bottom remembers it too.

My mom noticed that I was no longer in her eyesight. So, she went outside looking for me. She searched the entire apartment complex. While searching, she noticed some of the children I had been playing with and inquired if they had seen me. To my surprise, they snitched and told her where I was located. Look at that. Sometimes, the people that rat you out are your (own) friends. I had gone into my friend's house who had the barbies. She invited me, and it would have been wrong not to go. Right? The story didn't end too well for the home team (Team Annette).

After asking around the neighborhood, my mother finally discovered my location. I was playing in my friend's room when her mother came to the door and said my mother had arrived to pick me up. You know my eyes were as big as two golf balls. Let me tell you. It was a slowwww and longgggg walk home. I trailed my mother, with tears rolling down my face knowing what my fate would be once I got home. I will let you use your imagination on how the story ends. Here is a hint. I could not sit down for a while.

My mom would tell this (same) story describing a couple sitting on a bench as we passed. The couple said, "aww, look at that pretty little girl crying, and her mom is not waiting for her." They gave my mom the meanest stare. They did not realize that I was the disobedient one (no matter how pretty I was).

Despite stories like these, I enjoyed great times while living in New York. I remember going to my fraternal grandparents' house in Jamaica Queens. I referred to them as Nana and big Danny. I remember learning how to ride my bike there and playing with my half-sister Deborah who was two years older than me. My Nana would spoil me so much. Anything I asked for, she would give to me without question. On one occasion, I was visiting. She was cooking dinner. As she began preparing rice from a bag, I told her, "my mom doesn't cook that kind of rice. She only cooks Uncle Ben converted rice." Can you believe that she left and bought Uncle Ben converted rice? I sure was being a brat back then.

My Aunt Linda, my father's sister, always said, "Mom, why do you spoil her so much?" My Nana would answer, "because she is my baby, I can spoil her as much as I want." Of course, with my inside voice, I agreed. She can spoil me as much as she wants. It was only in Jamaica Queens that I got away with spoiled brat behavior because that did not happen in Cunningham Heights. In Cunningham Heights, I was the opposite of a spoiled brat. I was respectful. I had manners. I was a good student. Bernice would not have it any other way.

My childhood was good yet sometimes challenging. I had a loving mother and the best grandparents any child could have. I have great memories of us always eating dinner together. My family looked like the Cosbys at the dinner table. The table was set with fine china, beautiful silverware, glasses (not crystal), and different foods were spread on the table on platters and in bowls. We would say our grace, serve our food, and discuss the day's events. My days were not much since all I (mainly) did was attend school.

Nonetheless, I was a social butterfly. Imagine that! My report cards stated, "Annette is a sweet little girl who likes to visit with her neighbors." My mother and grandmother made sure that I was always polite and used proper manners. Around the dinner table is where I learned about family values & table etiquette. Etiquette included, but was not limited to, no talking with food in your mouth, no elbows on the table, no singing at the table, sitting up straight, eating all your food, and asking to be excused from the table when done eating. After making it through the table etiquette and dinner, desserts would be served. Desserts were the best part of the meal for me. To this present day, I like a little something sweet after dinner. After dinner, it was bath time and then bedtime. I loved them both. Bath time was when I got an opportunity to play in the tub. I would say, "Mommy can I have some bubbles, please?" "Yes, you can," she would reply. Then into the tub comes Mr. Bubbles from the big pink bottle. She would also use dishwashing detergent if we were out of Mr. Bubbles. I would play for 30 minutes, although it seemed like five, before mom advised that bath time was over.

Next, bedtime, and I enjoyed this too. Strange, right? Not really. I like to call my liking of bedtime unique. My mom would enter the room, tuck me in, and then read (me) a bedtime story. My favorite book was Green Eggs & Ham by the famous Dr. Suess. She read this book so often that I would repeat every word with her as she read.

She also had a big book that was about 4 inches thick. The book had 365 stories. Thus, you had a story for every day of the year. Now and then, she would grab the big book because I am sure she was tired of reading Green Eggs and Ham.

My mom was between the age of 24 to 25 years old during this time. I could only imagine if my dad had been sitting at the dinner table sharing the events of his day. I can only imagine if my dad had been there to pour my bubbles into the tub. I can only imagine if my dad was there to tuck me in and read Green Eggs and Ham. That's just it. *I can only imagine*.

I thank God for my mom, my grandmother, and the silent partner, "papa," my wonderful grandfather. My mom was such a special lady. Looking over my life, I can also attest that she was a great mom who did her best with what she had.

Then the Lord formed man from the dust of the ground and breathed into his nostrils the breath of life, and the man became a living soul.
Genesis 2:7 ~ New International Version

Humility is the fear of the Lord; its wages are riches and honor and life.
Proverbs 22:4 ~ New International Version

Who Am I?

At the tender age of 15, I was a scared and confused teenager attempting to understand life. Imagine that. I missed my father, although I never knew him. Maybe it was just the idea of me not having an earthly father. I endured the things that teenagers usually go through. All teenagers typically experience raging hormones and believe no one understands them. Sometimes I felt so alone. I had plenty of friends and a large family. Yet, loneliness was real.

Speaking of family, I have one particular uncle named Joe. He spent so much time with me that he was more like a father figure. He spoiled me too. He would drive me to Tampa from Tarpon Springs, approximately 30-36 miles, to get a dozen Krispy Kreme doughnuts. OMG! If that "Hot Now" sign were on, I would think I had died and gone to heaven. On one occasion, I recall eating so many of them that I (literally) got sick from all the sugar. Uncle Joe taught me how to drive. He would help me with my homework. He even tried to teach me how to play chess without much luck.

We played board games and, when bored, took long drives anywhere. Once, we ended up in Ft. Lauderdale. I just loved hanging out with him.

As close as we were, I still felt I could not talk to him or any of my family members about certain issues. I thought that they would not understand the emptiness that I felt. Even I did not understand it. All I knew was that I was tired of crying and not knowing why. I would lie in bed at night in a fetal position with my whole body covered with a soft purple and white fleece blanket that my grandmother had given me. My pillows were soaked from my tears, and I wished that I was not alive. I wished that I could escape and be with my father. The weird thing is that even with these thoughts going through my mind, I never thought about taking my life. I just wanted to be taken up in a whirlwind like Elijah. No one would miss me, right?

I often wondered, why am I here? Who am I? Really? I was raised in the church but did not understand what it meant. All I knew was I had to have my hinny in church EVERY Sunday. So, allow me to share one of my most memorable experiences in church.

One evening, my home church, Mt Moriah A.M.E. in Tarpon Springs, Florida, was hosting a special church event. I attended the service, as usual, not expecting to get anything out of it except a bunch of laughs as my cousins, close friends, and I would often do as we sat in the back of the church. We did not pay any attention to the preached word. Instead, we would make fun of the ladies with those fancy hats ranging from small pill box shapes to large floppy sizes that prevented you from seeing the person in front of you. But then, some hats seemed to have flower gardens on the side. You name it. We would spot it.

The ladies were not the only ones that gained our laughter. First, the deacons would sing those long, drawn-out songs that put people to sleep. Then, the pastor yelled and screamed. It made us wonder if God was hard of hearing. Sister so-and-so repeats, "Amen, Pastor." Brother so-and-so repeats, "Preach, Preacher, Preach." Little did I know, I was about to experience something that I had never experienced, nor would I ever forget.

The service started with singing, praying, and scriptures being read. Then, more singing, and finally, we received the preached word. I cannot remember what the evangelist preached, but she called a couple of my friends and me to the altar. She began to prophesy over us. Suddenly, I heard someone tell me to run. I ran to the back of the church. I turned around and ran back to the front. Then, I ran to the back and again from the back to the front. As I returned to the front of the church, she took my hands, looked me in the eyes, and said, "I see you speaking in front of a large crowd in a stadium. People from all around the world will come to hear you speak." That was the night that I gave my life to Christ.

Once I gave my life to Christ, I started to feel better. I still had moments because I did not fully understand what it meant. However, I knew that God was with me. I could always feel his presence. I always knew something was special about me, but not sure what. Even at a young age, I was considered trustworthy and could advise others.

As I got older, I began to build my relationship with God by studying His word, attending Sunday School, Bible Study, Church, and listening to televangelists. I began to understand that God's plan for me was for me. Yet, I am still waiting on my speaking engagements. I know that God always keeps his promises. He knows what He has purposed for my life, and I realize that everything occurs in His time.

I believe God is preparing me for something. Although, honestly, sometimes I am afraid. Nonetheless, I remember someone saying, "do it scared. God will be with you because you are doing it for Him." So, until that time, I will keep preparing and positioning myself to be on that stage.

Who Am I?

- ➢ I Am a Child of the most-high God!
- ➢ I Am Chosen!
- ➢ I Am Loved!
- ➢ I Am saved by His Blood!
- ➢ I Am bought with a price!
- ➢ I Am covered by His Blood!
- ➢ I Am created in His image!
- ➢ I Am above and not beneath!

> ➤ I Am the head and not the tail!
> ➤ I Am Victorious!
> ➤ I Am healed by His stripes!
> ➤ I Am no longer confused or afraid!
> ➤ I Am no longer bound!
> ➤ I Am Free!

With the spirit of the living God now living within me, I know who I am.

You, dear children, are from God and have overcome them, because the one who is in you is greater than the one who is the world.

1 John 4:4 ~ New International Version

Charity Starts At Home

Someone once said charity starts at home. I am a true believer that it does. At least, for me, it did. As far as I remember growing up, I have always lived with my grandparents and mom. There were maybe 4 ½ years of my life that I did not live with my grandparents. However, I lived with my grandparents, James Freeman & Irene "Charity" Brown, for most of my childhood and young adult life. They were the best grandparents a girl like me could have. I thank God for choosing them for me and me for them. So, come with me as I share my gift of Irene Charity Brown.

Irene Charity Brown was the epitome of her name. She was affectionately known to her children, grands, great-grands, and great-great-grands as "Mother." To her nieces, nephews, and close friends, she was known as "Annie." To her siblings, she was known as "Sister." To her church family, she was known as "Mother Brown" and "The Girl Can't Help It." And last but not least, to her adorable husband, James Freeman Brown, she was known as "Mommy."

When Mother was growing up, she was a strong black woman that stood about 5 feet tall. She had long black hair, pecan brown skin, nicely shaped, beautiful white teeth, a smile that would light up a room, and a tongue that would light you up (lol). She was an extremely wise woman who was strong in her beliefs. Mother loved her family and never met a stranger. She would open her doors to anyone. Watching my grandmother live her life just as she preached helped mold me into the hospitable person I am. She never judged anyone, nor did she look down on them. Mother helped any and everyone she could. She started the "No Child Left Behind" slogan long before it became popular. She always spoke with wisdom as well as humor. She would give it to you straight with no chaser. She said, "If you don't want to hear the truth, don't ask me."

You could talk to her about anything and never worry about hearing it again. She was a perfect example of confidentiality. She taught and often reminded me to treat people the way I want to be treated, even if they don't deserve it. Why? Your reward from God is far better than anything you can get from man, and one thing is for sure,

God does not sleep. He sees all your deeds - good, bad, or indifferent. She introduced me to God, and I thank her for that. She taught me to be independent almost to a fault. I remember her telling me, "You are too independent for your own good." I laughed and said, "Well, that's what you taught me."

My grandmother was not only a wife, mother, grandmother, great-grandmother, and great-great-grandmother; she was also a lawyer, marriage counselor, guidance counselor, ATM, loan officer, doctor, midwife, nurse, cook, chauffeur (without pay), and I cannot leave out the title of the regulator. She had a very kind and gentle spirit. I pray I am half the woman to people who come into my life as she was to me.

My grandfather, James Freeman Brown, was known as "PaPa." He was the silent partner, but to know him was to love him. He never had much to say, but he made it count when he did. He was loving and abundantly kind, and he loved his grandchildren. But, most of all, he loved the Lord. PaPa was very smart, and I loved talking to him.

He was born in 1915. Thus, he saw a lot during his lifetime. I recall receiving an assignment to complete a class report on the Great Depression. All I had to do was interview him. He shared so many stories. When I was done putting the report together, the result was an "A."

He was drafted into the military and could not finish school, but when he was done with his tour, he returned home and graduated from high school. I have his original High School Diploma. He worked hard for the New York Sanitation Department for 20 years before retiring in 1969. Post-retirement, he and my grandmother moved back to Florida.

As I have mentioned, all the accolades about my grandmother - my grandfather has just as many. He lived his life being a man that feared God. He was kind, gentle, supportive, compassionate, a silent partner, and most of all, he was my grandmother's backbone. He believed that whatever Mommy wanted, Mommy got it." They both were family-oriented. They adopted one of their great-nieces to ensure she would be raised with her family. I remember they would load up the camper truck or station wagon, whichever vehicle they had at the time, with all the grands, sometimes nieces and nephews, and the baby. Then, off we went to a park, Walt Disney World, or to visit family in Sarasota. I always enjoyed every minute I spent with my grandparents, and I miss them both dearly.

My grandfather spoiled my grandmother and was a great role model to me. You would think that with the example that he had given me, I would have made better choices when it came to dating, but that's for another chapter. However, I did observe the way that he treated my grandmother, and I knew that without a shadow of a doubt, his mannerisms were how I wanted my husband to treat and support me.

I thank God that He allowed me to reciprocate the kindness that they both shared with me to each of them. I was blessed to be one of their caregivers, helping to care for them in their last days. My grandfather lived to be 96 years old. The Lord called him home on April 12, 2011. My grandmother lived to be 92. The Lord called her home on May 5, 2017. They lived long and prosperous lives in my eyes. May God rest their souls.

Start children off on the way they should go, and even when they are old, they will not turn from it.

Proverbs 22:6 ~ New International Version

Looking For Love In All The Wrong Places

Did you know that there is such a thing called "Fatherless Daughter Syndrome?" Yes. Fatherless Daughter Syndrome is real. Fatherless Daughter Syndrome is a disorder of the emotional system that leads to repeated dysfunctional relationship decisions with men as girls grow up. The dysfunction mainly appears in the areas of trust and self-worth. In addition, the syndrome creates a lack of emotional attachment between a daughter and her father in his absence, be it death, divorce, abuse, addiction, abandonment, or incarceration. Finally, it is beginning to make sense. I am beginning to understand what this Fatherless Daughter Syndrome is all about. I hope that by the time you read this chapter and this book, you will gain an understanding of it too.

As I hash out things in my mind and look back over my life, I made a few decisions that can be attributed to this syndrome. Three significant relationships fall into the definition of Fatherless Daughter Syndrome, especially the part that speaks about dysfunctional decision-making. I have had more than three relationships, but I decided to focus on the three that helped shape my life and contributed to who I am today. The relationships may have been dysfunctional, but they were not in vain. Each of them has taught me lifelong lessons. I will not make them out to be the bad guys. Yet, I am sharing insight into these relationships because my decision-making surrounding them had significant implications in my life as I went through life without my father, Danny.

Where do I start? The beginning. I have changed the names to protect the innocent. I will refer to them as Mr. Mac Daddy, Mr. Smoother Operator, and Mr. Rico Suave. They were wrong for me yet right for my growth. I consider the relationships with these three men, respectively, as the building blocks for, The House of Annette Elease Elliott (my life).

We all know that when you are building a house, you must have a strong solid foundation. But, unbeknownst to me, I had a very strong and solid foundation that God had already established.

"For I know the plans I have for you declares the Lord, plans to prosper you and not to harm you, plans to give hope and a future."
Jeremiah 29:11 ~ New International Version

Let's explore the relationships that resulted from my bout with Fatherless Daughter Syndrome and contributed to the building of "The House of Annette."

Mr. Mac Daddy

I always looked forward to my summer vacation in Tarpon Springs, Florida. While in Tarpon Springs, I had the opportunity to spend time with my southern family and friends. I had to be about six years old when I started flying to Florida from New York alone. I remember the first time I flew alone. I got to sit in the front of the airplane with the stewardess (that's what they were called back then). I sat there like a big girl, and they took good care of me. I loved receiving extra snacks. I felt so special when I received a set of delta wings to place on my jacket.

A Fatherless Daughter

The 4th summer in my travels to Florida was the summer of all summers. I was nine years old. At this stage of my life, playing outside was not a foreign language or a death punishment, as some children see it today. I enjoyed playing outside because doing so was not too popular in New York. Tarpon Springs was a small town, and everyone knew everyone. All the neighborhood children, including my family and friends, played outside. Some were on roller skates, some on bikes, and some were hanging out. Some girl's games were hopscotch, jumping rope, and little Sally Walker, to name a few. Unfortunately, these outdoor games are foreign to today's children. Most would rather remain indoors, play video games, or watch television. They have no interest in engaging in outdoor games.

This particular day we were all playing outside when one of my cousins brought me a message saying that this young boy from the neighborhood named Mac Daddy liked me. He wanted to know if I liked him. I said, "yuck, no, I don't like that fat boy." That was the end of that. We returned to playing without missing a beat. After that, I never gave Mac Daddy another thought.

A few more years and a few more summer trips passed. Finally, my family decided to relocate back to Florida permanently during the winter break of 1973. Thus, I completed my 5th-grade year in the warm weather of Florida. Thank God. My family's relocation to Florida did not have much bearing on me because I had already established friends and family. During this time, elementary schools only went to the 5th grade. Then, the junior high school covered 6th through 8th grade. Finally, the high school years covered 9th through 12th grade.

At 16, during my junior year in high school, I discovered that there was not much for teenagers to do in the small town of Tarpon Springs. It was not unusual for us to take walks around our neighborhood. One day my cousin and I were taking our afternoon walk when a yellow mustang started to drive slowly beside us. I was walking closest to the driver's side of the car. Wouldn't you know it was Mr. Mac Daddy? However, he was no longer the "yuck fat boy" anymore. He was an 18-year-old, nicely built, rather handsome man with caramel complexion skin and natural curly black hair. I began looking at him in a completely different light and thinking, he's not so bad after all. He has lost all that baby fat. I could work with him now (LOL).

I would have never imagined that we would end up together as a couple. But, as life would have it, we began to see each other seriously. Our time together seemed to pass by. I guess what they say is true. Time flies when you're having a good time. We had as much fun as any young couple could. As I learned about my father, Mr. Mac Daddy always dressed nicely and had a nice car. Oh, and yes, the ladies loved him, but not as much as I did. Boy, was I wrong.

During our dating time, I would often visit him at his parent's house, and from time to time, he would come to my house for a visit. I remember this one particular day as if it were yesterday. I am unsure of the exact date. However, I believe it was in January 1979. I went to visit him at his parent's house. When I entered the house, his parents were sitting in the living room watching TV. So, I sat on the sofa and joined them in watching TV. After sitting there for a little while, Mr. Mac Daddy appeared and said, "let's go outside." I want to talk to you about something." We walked outside, but this day would be different from any other day. We walked around the side of the house, heading towards the backyard to sit on the back porch. Suddenly, he stopped at the side of the house and said, "I want to have a baby. I want someone to carry on my name." I looked at him like he had three heads and said, "you what?" On cue, he repeated the same sentences. "I want to have a baby. I want someone to carry on my name." Get this.

I had (just) turned 17 years old in December of my senior year in high school. At that time, I was only planning to be an airline stewardess. My mother had recently paid part of my tuition for the school I would attend after graduation. The plan was to take a few classes locally, then relocate to Miami to Delta Training School for hands-on training. The recruiter told me that being a stewardess was like being a doctor. I would always be on call. That was no issue because I had no responsibilities and loved traveling and flying.

After all, I had been flying since age six. I was looking forward to flying all over the world for free.

Finally, I responded. "I'm too young to have a baby." He replied, "well, if you don't have my baby, someone else will." In my young, naïve mind, I would not let that happen. I soon stopped taking my birth control pills, and within a month, I was pregnant. WOW! If this was not the face of Fatherless Daughter Syndrome and dysfunctional decision-making, I do not know what to call it.

As you can probably imagine, my mother's money went down the drain. My plans of being an airline stewardess flew out the window. No pun intended. Now we have a baby on the way. Pink or blue. When is the baby due?

The infamous baby requested to carry his name was scheduled to arrive in November 1979. Let me tell you. 1979 was a busy year for me.

> I got pregnant in February.
> I graduated from high school in June and,
> I gave birth to a baby in November.

Now back to the story. November 11th was the due date for the baby. November 11th came and went.

November 15th – no baby. November 20th - no baby. Thanksgiving was on November 22nd, and I enjoyed the holiday. However, on November 25th – no baby. Early Monday morning, on November 26, 1979, I began to feel a pain in my stomach that I had never felt before. The time had finally come. I was going to Dunedin Mease Hospital to deliver the baby that would carry on Mr. Mac Daddy's family name. I was extremely excited and scared, but it turned out that the baby was not ready to make an appearance. I was sent back home—what a bummer.

While at home, they told me to walk and not eat. Well, one out of two was not bad. I walked up and down Overlea Street until the pain came back. This time, the pain arrived more frequently. So off we went back to the hospital. This visit had to be the one during which our baby would come. Finally, at 10:08 pm, the infamous baby weighing in at 9lbs, 10ozs, and 21 inches long had (finally) arrived. **She** was beautiful. **She** looked like a baby doll with a head full of silky black hair. **She** had a light complexion and beautiful brown eyes. Yes, folks, it was a girl.

Well, so much for carrying on the family name. We were very proud young parents and still trying to figure life out. We tried to make our little family work, but it was not in the stars. After about four years of breaking up and making up, breaking up and making up, me thinking that I was in love and not wanting my daughter to be raised without her father, we finally accepted that we could not fit a square peg into a circle. We both decided this relationship was not going to work. We parted ways.

After the breakups and years of us growing and learning (I can honestly say), we became close friends. Weirdly, Mr. Mac Daddy became more of a big brother and a protector over me. I eventually realized that he did want me to experience happiness and to have someone in my life that treated me with respect and love. I may have made a bad decision, but God blessed me with the perfect gift of my beautiful baby girl, Ronisha Comia.

Having her made me grow up fast. I was now responsible for someone else. A little person depended on me. I learned how to be a responsible and independent adult through the relationship. When she was nine months old, I went to school to learn bookkeeping and record keeping. I worked two jobs, bought a car from one of my neighbors, and provided for my baby in the best way possible. When she turned two years old, I gained employment with the Pinellas County Tax Collector. I thought, "Princess Ronisha, we're on our way now."

Every good and perfect gift is from above, coming down from the Father of lights, who does not change like shifting shadows.

James 1:17 ~ New International Version

Mr. Smooth Operator

I am now 22 years old with a four-year-old daughter, and I am still seeking and trying to figure out my life as a single parent. I would sometimes hang out in the parks on Sundays in Clearwater. The hang-out location was called "Chunky Sunday." At Chunky Sunday, most young adults, teenagers, and children would gather to socialize and listen to music. Some young men would be on their motorcycles and in their supped-up cars. Others would sit around talking and telling stories (and lies). The young ladies would walk around the park with their children. Others would linger around the playground, and some sat on the hoods of their cars, watching people.

One day I was out at the park and caught the eye of Mr. Smooth Operator. We exchanged numbers and went on a couple of dates. We enjoyed movies, dancing, and hanging out with other friends. As time passed, we decided to take it to the next level and date each other exclusively. We spent more and more time together and eventually decided to move in together. Look at that. Fatherless Daughter Syndrome strikes again. Wouldn't you know it? We discussed starting a family. Honestly, I did not want my children to have different fathers, but this was not an option. Well, at least not without conflict, if you know what I mean. At age 24, with Ronisha being almost six years old, I thought it was now or never.

After more discussion, I discovered I was "in the family way" again. It was January 1985. My second bundle of joy was scheduled to arrive around October 15th. I must say that my second pregnancy was great. I only gained 24 lbs, and the doctors were very pleased because, unlike my first pregnancy, I gained 50 lbs. Since this was my second pregnancy, I wanted to know the baby's sex. Thus, as soon as I was able to find out, I did. It's a girl.

Although the second pregnancy was great, the support from Mr. Smooth Operator was not. I began to wonder how he felt now that the talks of starting a family had turned into reality. There was much doubt. However, as time passed, I made the best of the situation. Yes, this was Fatherless Daughter Syndrome mentality at its best. On October 17th at 7:18 pm EST, my second gift from God made her debut. She was just as beautiful as Ronisha. She came in, weighing 7 lbs, 6 ozs, and 19 inches long. She, too, had a head full of hair, beautiful brown eyes, and a light pecan complexion. She was the perfect little angel. She was named Ikesha LaCole.

I must give credit where credit is due. When Ikesha was born, Mr. Smooth Operator was very attentive to her. He went to every doctor's appointment with us and undressed her in preparation for the doctor's arrival in the room. Mr. Smooth Operator was such a proud father. He would take her everywhere with him. Our relationship had ups and downs, but we stayed together.

I treated our relationship as if we were married, again, attempting to be a family. I would get up every morning, cook breakfast, prepare everyone's lunch, clean up, get the kids ready for school (elementary and daycare), and then work all day. When I returned home, I cooked dinner, cleaned up, helped Ronisha with her homework, got Ikesha ready for bed, and prepared their belongings for the next day. Afterward, I prepared for bed, slept, and rose the next day. Repeat.

This routine went on for a couple of years. Mr. Mac Daddy and Mr. Smooth Operator had something in common. They had a thing for the ladies, and the ladies had a thing for them. An old saying states, "you live, and you learn." Well, that's how it is supposed to be. I guess I was a slow learner (ha-ha). The cycle repeats. Mr.

Smooth Operator began to act strange. Our relationship was strained. Two children were born while we were still together and outside our relationship. Mr. Smooth Operator told me all kinds of fabricated stories. Some of them were so farfetched that I will not bother to repeat them. However, it had reached the point that our relationship had to end.

I was a little older and a little more mature when this relationship ended, so it did not have the same ending as I had with Mr. Mac Daddy. What was the difference? When my relationship ended with Mr. Mac Daddy, I was younger, and the breakup did not affect me the same. I (really) had terrible feelings toward Mr. Smooth Operator. I was hurt and scared at the same time. If only I had a father to give me words of wisdom. I needed fatherly encouragement. If I had my father's guidance, maybe one of these relationships would have turned out differently. I guess that's something we will never know. Yet, again, I may have made the wrong decision, but God blessed me *a second time* with a beautiful little girl. Thank you, Lord, for my blessings!

Every good and perfect gift is from above, coming down from the Father of lights, who does not change like shifting shadows.

James 1:17 ~ New International Version

<u>Mr. Rico Suave</u>

Here I go again. I am 28 years old and living as a single parent with a 4-year-old and a 10-year-old. I was working a full-time job from 8:00 am to 5 pm. Additionally, I worked a part-time job in the evenings and sometimes on the weekend. Thank God for my mother and my grandparents. They were indeed life savers. I will share more about them later.

Although I worked two jobs, I found time to spend with my daughters, family, and friends. One Saturday night, my (home)girls and I were heading out for a night out on the town. We planned to engage in a bit of bar hopping, dancing, and just having clean fun. By the night's end, we were in the last nightclub, known as "The Fountain." The Fountain is where I met Mr. Rico

Suave. He was a nice-looking young man. He was dressed nicely, and he had a little swag about him. I was hanging with my (home)girls when he made his way to me. We had already made eye contact a few times. He asked, "Would you like to dance?" I replied, "sure." We danced through a few songs, and then he asked if I wanted a drink. I replied, "yes, I would like a soda." He said, "a soda?" I said, "yes, I don't drink." He said, "you don't drink? Ok." After receiving my soda, we talked and danced for the rest of the night and exchanged phone numbers before leaving the nightclub.

After about a month or so of hanging out, we decided to take it to the next level, which meant dating each other exclusively. Well, exclusive to each other is what I thought we would be. By the way, did I mention he was 22 years old with a 6-year-old son? I was six years older than him, but I (certainly) did not meet the definition of being a cougar. I believe that if you are eight years older, you qualify. LOL.

As our relationship grew, we appeared to have a blended family. We all got along well; he and my girls, me and his son, Devon. Early in our relationship, we would have long talks to get to know each other. I shared my deepest thoughts and feelings, especially regarding infidelity. I shared that in my last relationship, two children were conceived while we were still together, and a few other extra affairs. I also expressed how I did not want to go down that same road. He assured me that was not going to happen. I had no idea what I was about to get myself into, and the cycle continued.

As time went on, we spent more time together. However, Mr. Rico Sauvé's behavior began to change. I realized that Mr. Mac Daddy and Mr. Smooth Operator had the same things in common, and Mr. Rico Suave also had the same characteristics. I (later) realized that I chose to be with each of them. Do you recognize the pattern? They loved the ladies, and the ladies loved them. Here I go again, making another dysfunctional decision. It was the same movie, but with different characters. I saw all the signs. All the red flags rose on the left and right like popcorn. I chose to ignore them ALL. After all, I thought I was in love. I made excuses, saying things like, "he is young" or "he will change." Do these phrases sound like anything you have ever whispered about someone you loved? Well, he did not change. Mr. Rico Suave had a baby on the way when we got together, and a 6-year-old daughter, which we later discovered was his. The list goes on. There were three additional babies, of which one lived with us (Sterling). I cannot count the number of disrespectful phone calls and confrontations I witnessed. I had to end it. Enough was enough. Here is the funny or (maybe) not-so-funny fact of the situation - it took me ten years to reach the point of enough.

Over time, I grew close to his sons. I considered them to be my sons too. It was harder for me to leave them than for me to leave Mr. Rico Suave himself. Yet, they were his sons, and I could not take them with me for more reasons than one.

My relationship with Mr. Rico Suave ended better than with Mr. Smooth Operator but not as good as with Mr. Mac Daddy. Thus, I guess it landed somewhere in the middle. I may have made another wrong relationship decision, but I gained two sons with whom I keep in contact from time to time.

I thank God that He showed me what true love is. It was Him (God) all along. I was looking for love in all the wrong places. You have received a snapshot of my three major dysfunctional decisions. This is Fatherless Daughter Syndrome.

God was with me through them all, whether I recognized Him or not. He proved that even when I was not faithful to Him, He was always faithful to me. God chose me, and I accepted Him as a teenager. After that, I just had to build my relationship with Him, and I am so glad I did.

I can honestly say that I have no hard feelings toward any of my "building blocks." I am good friends with Mr. Mac Daddy and his wife. I am friends with Mr. Smooth Operator and his wife, and I am friends with Mr. Rico Suave (I have only met his wife a few times, but all is good). Who knows. We may all hang out together one day.

On another note, I would like to thank Mr. Mac Daddy, Mr. Smooth Operator, and Mr. Rico Suave for helping to build the house of Annette

Elease Elliott. You know who you are. You have helped in building a strong, black, independent woman. You have taught me not to settle for anything less than (what) God has for me. You have made me more aware of self-value, and you all have helped to equip me to be the best wife I could ever be for my "Knight in Shining Amour."

Trust in the Lord with all your heart and lean not on your own understanding; in all your ways submit to Him, and He will make your paths straight.

Proverbs 3:5-6 ~ New International Version

Thank You Jesus

Let's talk about my "Knight in Shining Armour." But, before I begin, allow me to state this disclosure. It has been said that there are two sides to every story. I am sharing my side of the story as I remember it. If (and when) my Knight in Shining Armour decides to record his memories of our initial meet-up, he can share his story.

My Knight in Shining Armour came in and swept me off my feet. He did not arrive riding a white horse, but he was driving a 1998 black Dodge Neon. Isn't it amazing that you can remember every detail when you meet the love of your life? It was a Saturday evening. The date was June 10, 2000, to be exact. The Springtime Auxiliary Club (A social organization of which I was a member) was having a Pre-Father's Day dance at the Elks Lodge in Clearwater, Florida. My cousin and I were assigned to cover the entrance for the evening. The Elks Lodge was one of the main hangout spots in Clearwater, so we knew just about everyone that crossed the door's threshold.

As the night went on, more people began filling the building. Since it was a Father's Day dance, couples arrived in matching outfits. A few couples were color-coordinated. Others did not care. They were glad to be at the party. Single ladies came dressed conservatively, and some, not so much. Men arrived looking their "dapper" best. Others, not so much. Our post at the front entrance was fascinating, and we enjoyed a free fashion show.

Finally, the crowd began to slow down at the door, and I was getting a little hungry. So, I stepped away to purchase an order of chicken wings. Upon returning to my post, the crowd began to pick up again. Suddenly, three young men walked towards the door. Remember, we pretty much knew everyone that darted the door. As the three gentlemen came closer, my cousin and I looked at each other. We had never seen them before. They all were rather nice looking, but one caught my eye. Why? First, he was fine. Second, he had a smile that could light up a room (well, it did for me). Third, he had dimples, and I love dimples. Fourth, he stood about 5'9" with a medium build, a low haircut, and a fair complexion. I was never too keen on light-skinned men. Men with lighter skin seemed to be into themselves, in my opinion. He looked like he was of Spanish descent, maybe from the Dominican Republic or Puerto Rican. He wore a white turtleneck shirt, blue jeans, and white sneakers. But, hey, I was not (really) paying that much attention. Right?

One by one, each of them made their way through the entrance and paid their entry fee. The gentleman that caught my eye was the first to pay. As he stood waiting for his friends to pay, he started a conversation with me. He said, "excuse me, may I have a piece of your chicken?" I responded, "sure." He reached over and grabbed a piece of chicken. He did not grab any old piece. Instead, he took the biggest part of the wing, the drumstick. And not only did he grab the drumstick, but he had the nerve to dip his piece of chicken in my ranch dipping sauce. I gave him a strange look. However, it was ok because he was (kind of) cute after all. After getting his chicken, he asked me what I was drinking. I replied, "Remy red and pineapple juice." (No soda this time.) I asked, "why are you going to buy me a drink?" He said, "yes." I said, "ok." Then off he went into the lodge.

Time was moving, and the music was grooving. I continued to sip my drink, but my glass soon became empty. I asked my cousin to go inside and tell the young man I was talking to that I was ready for my drink. She proceeded into the lodge. After a few minutes, she returned with our drinks. I was all excited and wondered what he had said to her. So, I asked, "what did he say?" She replies, "I did not remember what he looked like, so I just went to the bar and got our drinks." All I said while shaking my head was, "oh my goodness." I guess it is true. If you want a job done right, you must do it yourself. So, off I went into the lodge to find the handsome stranger. It did not matter that I had the drink my cousin had purchased. I wanted the drink that was promised to me by him.

I circled the lodge and finally spotted him sitting at a table. I passed him as if I did not see him, but then I stopped, backed up, leaned over, and whispered in his ear, "my throat is dry." Then, without missing a beat, I walked away without looking back. Within ten minutes, my drink was delivered by the waitress. That is what I am talking about - mission accomplished.

As the night ended, I went back inside. Lo and behold, whom do I see? You guessed it – my Knight in Shining Armour. He asked me for my phone number. I told him I do not give out my phone number, but I would take his. He gave me his home and work number. We said our goodbyes and went our separate ways. The next day I called the number to ensure he had not given me a bogus phone number. He had not.

When I called, he was spending the day with his sons. Yet, over the next few weeks, we occasionally communicated via phone but never saw each other in person. Over time, we stopped talking. Three months elapsed.

One day while at work, one of my co-workers transferred a call to me. I answered and said, "thank you for calling the Pinellas County Tax Collector's office. This is Annette. How may I help you?" The following words I heard floored me. "I want you to drop your pants and bend over. I am going to spank your butt. Why haven't I heard from you?" All I could do was laugh. My Knight in Shining Armour was on the phone. From that day forward, we have never stopped talking.

After the call to my workplace, we spoke on the phone a few more times and (finally) decided to go on a date. We made plans to meet at 9:00 pm at the Bicycle Club (which no longer exists today). Anyone that knew me knew that my mother and I were very close. She was my ride-or-die chick. Thus, she would be with me if I went anywhere. I remember telling my grandmother, as my mom and I were getting ready to go out, that I was going to meet her grandson. I did not realize that this statement would turn out to be true. There is POWER in the tongue.

We arrived at the nightclub around 9:30 pm. The club was crowded as it was Saturday night, one of their busier nights of the weekend. As we entered, the music played loudly, and people were dancing wildly, talking loudly, and drinking happily. The place was lively. I began to look around. There he was, looking as handsome as ever. I noticed that he was not alone either. I discovered that he had his brother with him. I guess we both had our escape plans. We mingled a little, had a couple of drinks, and began dancing. My mother had the first dance with him. In truth, she was running recon. LOL.

In summary, the first date went well. After that, we decided to see each other again. To fast forward, we did many things together to get to know each other. We watched movies and enjoyed dinners, dancing, and bowling. We even went to the Universoul Circus. The more time we spent together, we realized we had much in common.

I was coming out of a ten-year relationship with Mr. Rico Suave when I met him. I had a made-up mind that after all, I had gone through in past relationships, my next relationship would be all about me, not in a selfish way but in a way that I would not settle for anything and compromise my happiness for the sake of being with someone. I was not willing to make another dysfunctional decision surrounding a man.

The person for me would have to be in this thing as a partner. First, he must be a partner that wants to build a healthy life together - with

God as our guide. Second, he must be a partner willing to accept me for who I am and still love me unconditionally. Third, he must be a partner who allowed me to enjoy the fullness of life. Finally, he must be a partner with whom I could share the rest of my life. I had (also) decided that I would not live with, shack up, or be roommates with whom I dated unless we were making plans for marriage and we needed to save money. Unbeknownst to me, this would be easy because he had the same thoughts in mind. I told you we had a lot in common.

The more time we spent together, the more we wanted to be together. I had never met a man like this before. He was confident in himself and focused. He knew what he wanted out of life and, like me, knew what he did not want - DRAMA. He had an easy-going spirit which made me feel safe and secure.

I do not know if I mentioned this earlier, but he already had three children when we met. He was an outstanding father (from what I could tell). He would get his children every other weekend, and the attention he gave them was remarkable.

He had two boys. Gerric was 14, Jamell was 12, and a beautiful baby girl, Kaela, was nine months. He was so attentive to her. That was one of the many things that (really, really) impressed me about him. He did not mind changing her diapers, preparing her bottles, and playing with her. I could see by how he interacted with them that he was the one for me.

He showed me that family was significant to him. This characteristic was outstanding for me because I am genuinely a family-oriented person. Not only did he interact well with his children, but he also interacted well with mine, Ronisha and Ikesha, and my extended two children, Devon and Sterling, whom I helped to parent during my relationship with Mr. Rico Suave.

Time allowed our relationship to deepen. We spent a lot of time together, talking about everything. We talked about life, including children, work, and even the type of house or neighborhood we would like to live in. I recall one occasion when I stayed overnight at his place. The next morning, while he was in the shower, I prepared myself for work. I noticed a comb and brush on his dresser that was not mine, nor did I see them the night before. I immediately got an attitude. In my mind, I thought, "man, just when I thought I had met mister right, here comes this foolishness. I knew it was too good to be true". He came into the room after his shower. I was awkwardly quiet. I proceeded into the shower. I was boiling on the inside, but he did not know it. I showered, returned to the room, and began to get dressed. Surprise. My eyes roamed back toward the dresser. The comb and brush were gone. In my mind (again), I said, "no, this negro didn't." Now he is trying to play with my mind like I did not see what I know I saw. It's ok. I got some words for him. Imagine. I am having this conversation with myself.

I finished getting dressed, kissed him goodbye, and left as if nothing was wrong. He still had no idea how mad I was at this point. I did not have the nerve right then to talk to him, so I called him when I got into my car. In short, I said, "we need to talk." I had to get my thoughts and my speech together. He is going to get it. I don't know who he thinks he's playing with, I stated to myself.

He played basketball in a community league and had a game that night. So, after the game ended, I went to his place for the "BIG" talk. Well, in my mind, it was a BIG talk. I had all day and a nice little ride to prepare my good speech. I had all kinds of things to say, but I did not want to come across as a jealous and insecure woman. After all, I (really) liked him and did not want to scare him away.

After arriving at his place, he asked, "how was your day?" I responded, "it was good." We proceeded to watch TV. I am still trying to build up the nerve to start the conversation. In all honesty, I became a big chicken now that we were face to face. It was getting late, so I just launched into the conversation. "One thing I ask of you is that you never insult my intelligence." He replies slowly, "okay." I said, "you know when I realized I cared for you more than I thought?" He responded, "when"? I said, "when I saw that comb and brush on your dresser this morning, but after I got out of the shower, they were gone. I know that in all our conversations, we never said we were dating each other exclusively. Yet, as for me, you are the only one I am seeing, and that was my choice. I do not want to take it for granted that you are doing the same since we have not had that conversation". He smirked a little and said to me, "you mean to tell me you have been carrying this around with you all day?" I really wish you would have said something to me earlier. Yes, there was a comb and brush on my dresser. It belonged to a young lady that I was dating. They were under my bathroom sink for the longest time. However, I took them out to remind me to return them to her since she works down the street from me. I ask you to please not hold anything back from me. If something is on your mind, please tell me. We have not discussed dating each other exclusively, but you are correct. We can not take it for granted. By the way, I have been only seeing you as well. So, now we know where we stand. One more thing I want to say. I do not know where we are heading, but I can guarantee that if anything happens to us and we separate, it will not be because of another woman." I was blown away by that statement, and I believed him. THANK YOU, JESUS! My Knight in Shining Armour, Eric Douglas, had arrived.

We dated for about one year and decided to get married. Since we were not rich and had to pay for our wedding, we planned it for about one year and a half. We had a beautiful wedding with approximately 400 guests. Our reception is still being talked about after all these years.

I have learned that God must be in your relationship's front, middle, back, on top, and bottom for it to work. Together, we have learned the art of communicating in our relationship. I am proud to say that through these last 22 years, Eric and I have never argued. You may think I am lying, but God in heaven knows it is the truth. Now, don't get me wrong. There have been times that he has made me upset, and I am sure I have made him upset, but our disagreements have never reached a point where harmful words were exchanged.

I have also learned through this relationship that I may not be perfect, and he may not be perfect, but we are perfect for each other. Eric and I are in our 19th year of marriage, and we WILL live happily ever after with God continuing to be our guide.

A Fatherless Daughter

He: *How beautiful you are, my darling! Oh, how beautiful! Your eyes are like doves.*

She: *How handsome you are, my beloved! Oh, how charming! And our bed is verdant.*

Songs of Songs 1:15-16 ~ New International Version

God Is Not A Man That He Shall Lie

In September 2012, while living in Clearwater at my grandparent's home, my mom had an asthma attack that led to her being hospitalized and intubated. For those who may not know, intubation is the process of inserting a breathing tube through the mouth and into the airway. A tube is attached to a ventilator, commonly known as a respirator or breathing machine. The medical team also agreed to put her in a medically induced coma to keep her calm.

After three days on the ventilator, the medical team decided to take her off. She was breathing on her own, but she would not wake up. We all began to worry. Even her doctor was concerned and felt she should have been awake by now. Finally, on the fifth day, she opened her eyes. The first person she saw was my bonus dad, and she said to him, "you are so handsome." He immediately called me, and I returned to the hospital. I told my mom that she had given us all a scare. She stayed in the hospital for a few more days and was released to come home.

My mom was here in Clearwater on an assignment. Her assignment was to assist in caring for my aging grandparents. After (only) being out of the hospital for a week, she resumed her duties as a caregiver to Mother, my grandmother. Papa, my grandfather, transitioned on April 11, 2011. As the month went on, I could see she was not looking well. She began to lose weight and appeared unhealthy. I advised her to take a break from being a caregiver and go home to let my bonus dad, Hubert Lockhart, assume the caregiving duties. She did not want to leave my grandmother behind. Thus, she offered to take her with her. I had to change my role and become the parent-daughter. I told her, "No, you need to go home and take care of yourself." She finally agreed and went home to Ft. Lauderdale, Florida, in February 2013 without Mother in tow.

Eric and I drove her to Ft. Lauderdale in her car and rode the train back to Clearwater. She had a great time while living at home. My mom was able to get the well-deserved rest that she needed, as well as restoring her health. Finally, someone was able to take care of her for a change. We talked at least once daily, just like when she was in Clearwater.

Our church conducted a revival every spring and every fall, along with a Women's Conference in May. My mom made sure she was back in Clearwater to attend both revivals and the Women's Conference. She traveled by train to Clearwater one week before the Spring Revival and two weeks before the Women's Conference. During her stay, she and I had a great time. We did things that we had not done together in years. We shopped, watched movies, went to the beach, and enjoyed girl talks. Our time together was wonderful and filled with beautiful memories and treasured moments.

On a Thursday night before the spring revival, my mom stood in the doorway to my room. She said, "I just want to thank you and Eric for taking such good care of me," as tears rolled down her face. As I walked towards her, I said, "Mommy, why are you crying? You big waterbag, come give me a hug". We gave each other the biggest hug, and I ended our embrace with, "it is our pleasure and honor to take care of you."

The anticipation was finally over for the women of Mt. Olive AME Church. The Women In Unity Annual Women's Conference titled "The Women At The Well" was about to start. May 10, 2013, was the kickoff. The speaker brought a powerful message and prayed for every woman in the church, or so I thought. I will come back to that. The speaker prayed as the choir sang for what seemed like hours. The choir kept singing the words there is power in the name of Jesus to break every chain repeatedly. The words were engrained in my brain. The night ended on a spiritual high.

My mom and I headed home, but I needed to stop for gas. While at the gas station, my mom got out of the car and went into the store. She returned with a package of Oreo golden cookies. I finished pumping the gas, sat in the car, and she handed me the cookies stating that these should hold me until she could get to the store and buy me a replacement bag. Here is the back story to these cookies. Oreo golden cookies were my favorite cookies. I always kept a bag in my cookie drawer. Unbeknownst to me, my mom ate all my cookies while I was at work. Thus, her cookie gift to me was a small payback. She said, "I only ate two at a time." My response was, "well, how many times did you go in the kitchen?" After that, we just laughed as we always did together.

While continuing our ride home, my mom said, "Annette, the preacher did not pray for me." I said, "What? I thought she prayed for every woman. But maybe you did not need prayer because you are alright." She said, "I guess you are right." So, we continued home, laughing and talking.

It was time for us to head back to part two of the conference on Saturday morning. On Saturday's evening agenda was the performance of a short play based on the bible story, "The Woman at the Well." The play had a cast of five women and, of course, one man. Several family members were in the cast, including my niece Denae, Aunt Sandra, and myself.

Meanwhile, Saturday morning began with a continental breakfast followed by workshops and lunch. The attendees were blessed by a choreographed line dance from my Godson, Raymond. You should have seen us. We lined up to learn our new W.I.U. Shuffle to work off a few calories. The afternoon workshops concluded with an optional two-hour meditation period. This break gave women time to return home and prepare to return for the evening activities and our great debut.

My mom, grandmother, and aunt all went to the building next door, which is our Enrichment Center. The Enrichment Center had several rooms, and the big room was set up as a quiet room for meditation. The ambiance was very nice, with low lighting and soft music playing. The common area was for sitting and talking. The common area is where my family ended up.

Meanwhile, I was still in the building next door, preparing to leave to purchase flowers to give to all the mothers for Mother's Day. It was Mother's Day weekend. As I was getting things together, my aunt returned to the building, peeked inside, and said, "I need to take your mom to the house so she can get a breathing treatment." My mom had been laughing so much that it caused her to start coughing. I said, "ok." Then my aunt said, "I need to take your car." Since I was heading to Sam's Club to purchase the flowers, I advised that I would drop them off at home and return to pick them up before heading back to the church. A breathing treatment took 15-20 minutes and was sufficient time to complete my trip to Sam's Club.

Once in the car, I drove to Enrichment Center's back door and got out. However, I noticed they were all in the front of the building. As soon as I pulled into the parking space in front of the building, preparing to exit the car, a young girl came running out of the building with a phone in her hand. The following words that proceeded from her mouth would change my life forever. The young girl had a panicked look and shouted, "she's not breathing, she's not breathing." While in a state of confusion, I shouted, "who's not breathing?" The young girl said, "the lady inside." I proceeded immediately inside, and my mother was sitting in a chair, slumped to the right side, LIFELESS.

Everything that happened next appeared in slow motion. I took the phone from the young girl and began to talk to the 911 dispatcher. Where are the paramedics? I thought the fire station was only two blocks away. What was taking so long? What seemed like hours, I am sure, was only five minutes. When the paramedics arrived, I ran out of my shoe to go next door to let the first lady and my best friend, Serena, know what was happening. We all ran back to the building next door. The paramedics were working on her. All I could do was repeat JESUS, JESUS, JESUS. A paramedic came out and began asking medical questions about mom and if I knew she had gone into cardiac arrest. Of course, I answered no. He told me they had worked on her and got her heart to beat again but had to intubate her.

My husband and my daughters had arrived at the church by this time. Although I seemed alright on the outside, on the inside, I was a total wreck. In my mind, I felt that I had to be strong for everyone else. Silly me. They brought my mom out of the building on the stretcher. We all followed the ambulance to the hospital. While en route to the hospital, I called my bonus dad to inform him of what had happened. He was on the first thing smoking heading our way.

We arrived at the hospital before the ambulance, and the hospital personnel sat us in the family waiting room. There were about 6-7 of us in the room. We were waiting and waiting. Finally, the doctor came into the waiting room and said that she had been without oxygen to her brain for too long. My mom was in a coma. Finally, however, we were able to go in to see her.

When I stepped into the room, it was a sight I had seen twice before, but there was something different this time. I just felt it in my spirit. I recalled the conversation with my mom earlier that afternoon. The family gathered around her, and my pastor prayed for her, but I knew it was over. I was hurt, sad, shocked, and in disbelief. Yet, in the midst of it all - I had peace. I did not understand it then, but I would find out later.

I remained at the hospital the rest of that Saturday and spent the night. I did not want to leave her side. Finally, the doctors came in on Sunday and said that she had no brain activity and that we had to decide to take her off the machine. The decision to "pull the plug" was going to be one of the hardest decisions my dad and I would have to make. I prayed and made peace with the decision, but the final word had to come from my dad. He told me that whatever I wanted, he would be alright with it. He loved her so much and did not want to be the one to decide.

I departed briefly on Sunday to shower and change clothes. I returned directly back at the hospital. We waited another day because her brother was coming in from Ft. Lauderdale, and we wanted to give him a chance to see her before we took her off the machine. I spent Sunday night there and slept in the waiting room.

Around 2:00 am, the nurse approached me in the waiting room to say that I might want to come in because my mom's heart rate was dropping, and she could transition anytime. She was not off of the machine yet. Sunday passed into Monday, and my uncle was still en route. My kids and family had all returned to the hospital. My family, good friends, and church family are the best support system. At approximately 2:30 pm, my daughter Ronisha came to me and said, "mom, why don't you go home for a break? You don't have to stay gone long. If anything changes, we will call you." So, I went into the room and told my Mommie I would be back. I kissed her on the cheek and left the hospital.

Eric drove me home. When I got into the house, I laid in the bed in a fetal potion and let it all out with Eric holding me. About 30 minutes later, Eric's phone rang, and the person on the other line told him to return to the hospital. So, we flew (drove fast) back to the hospital. As I bent the corner, the first face I saw was my daughter Ronisha walking towards me with tears in her eyes, saying, "mommy, I am so sorry that I told you to go home. Bernie is gone." I grabbed my daughter, hugged her, and told her, "no, this is exactly how God wanted it to be. So, please do not feel bad." Unfortunately, my uncle did not make it in time. Yet, he was (only) 15 minutes away.

As the word spread of my mom's death, family and friends began to fill the waiting room. People were crying, praying, and talking. It seemed like my world had stopped for a moment. Of course, I could see and hear everyone, but it was surreal. Then one of my dear friends, who's like a brother, came to me and said the most profound words. He said, "Annette, I know that you will miss your mom but know that she will be with you everywhere you go because her blood runs through your veins." His words were so profound to me, and out of all the words of encouragement that I received, I have to say those were the best. Believe it or not, to this day (9 years later), I share those exact words with anyone who loses a mother or a father.

The homegoing celebration was phenomenal. There were so many people in attendance. Their presence was a testament to how she lived her life, full of love. May the life I live speak for me because my mom's life was the epitome of this song. I got the opportunity to share a few words at her wake, but it was during moments leading up to her homegoing that the Lord spoke to me. He said, "I am not a man that I shall lie. I told you I would not put more on you than you can bear. Remember about 25 years ago when your mom had that brain aneurysm? I could have taken her then, but you nor she was ready. You are ready now." His words were all I needed. I received that peace that surpasses all understanding, and I was not trying to understand. All I knew was that God was with me. Did it hurt? YES! Was I sad? YES! Do I miss her? YES! But through it all, I had PEACE!

God is not a man, so he does not lie. He is not human, so he should change his mind. Has he ever spoken and failed to act? Has he ever promised and not carried it through?

Numbers 23:19 ~ New Living Translation

God's Plan

As I look back over my life, I see now what I could not see then. God's plan is God's plan. I may have been raised without my father, but I had great role models. So, after you read the plans orchestrated only for me, I encourage you to reminisce over your life story. Rest confidently in knowing that the plans for your life have a purpose. God only does things decently and in order.

God knew then and now knows the plans He has for my life. God knew that I would be the daughter of Daniel & Bernice Elliott. God knew that my father would not see my face and that I would not see my father's face. God knew that I would have a half-sister, Deborah, who would die at 25 due to a drug overdose and that it would be at least ten years since I last saw her. God knew my mother would be a young bride and a mourning widow, all at the tender age of 18. God knew that she would become a single mom at 19. God knew I would spend most of my life with my wonderful grandparents. God knew I would be a teen mom and a mother to two beautiful daughters. God also knew I would go hard for my children, with or without their fathers. God knew that I would go through all the things that I went through. Even though God knew, he gave me free will to choose. Thus, some of the things I went through were due to my choices. God knew I would be blessed with a great work ethic, strong morals, and a kind spirit. God knew I would stay on my job for 35 years and retire young while in good health with a good pension. God knew I would struggle with (really) knowing who I was at some point in my life, but He also knew that I would figure it out once I established a REALationship with him.

God blessed me with a loving and forgiving heart. I cannot stay mad at anyone for long, and I always give others the benefit of the doubt. A compassionate heart could be viewed as a blessing and a curse. Why? Because I want everyone to get along. I want everyone to love one another, but it does not always work out. I had to realize that not everyone thinks like me and the real shocker was that not everybody likes me. Yet, God commands that I love them anyway. The word says we should not think more highly of ourselves than others. I did not think of myself more highly than others. However, I never thought that anyone would feel differently about me. But I guess it is true. If everyone likes you, something must be wrong with you. LOL. Everyone did not like Jesus, but He didn't let that stop Him from his assignment. He had to be about his father's business.

God knew He would send the man created for me to spend the rest of my days here on earth. God knew that we would have a bond like no other. God knew that Eric needed me just as much as I needed him. God knew that our families would become one. His friends would become my friends, and my friends would become his friends. God knew we would be the power couple He created us to be. Perfect? No. But we love God and are so grateful for all His blessings, teaching, and correcting.

God knew that the person reading this book would get a blessing from reading it, if not for themselves, but for someone suffering from "Fatherless Daughter Syndrome." So, you can give them words of encouragement. God knew I would be afraid and confused and struggle to write this book. Yet, God knew that He would be with me every step of the way, and I would complete this book in the timing He had predestined for me to finish. God knew because it was His plan!

God's Plan may be the last chapter of this book, but it is not the final chapter of my life.

"I am not saying this because I am in need, for I have learned to be content whatever the circumstances. I know what it is to be in need, and I know what it is to have plenty. I have learned the secret of being content in any and every situation, whether well fed or hungry, whether living in plenty or in want."

Philippians 4:11-12 ~ New International Version

Words Of Encouragement

As you recall and reflect on moments and seasons of your life, remember that God is always with you, even if you cannot feel Him. He said in His word that He would never leave or forsake you. It is essential to believe this promise with your mind and place it in your heart to move beyond circumstances that do not make sense at the time.

The mind and heart are two of the strangest organs we can have. They both are similar but separate. They are wonderful when they work together. Yet, they can be destructive when they do not.

Keep your faith. Never allow anything or anyone to destroy your faith. You are what and whom God says you are. You are fearfully and wonderfully made. You are the head and not the tail. You are above and not beneath. You are a lender and not a borrower.

Every day may not be a great day, but it is a blessed day. If you are reading this, then **YOU**, yes **YOU**, have been blessed by God. Your purpose is being fulfilled. Just ask God to show you His plans for your life. His plans may be different from what you have planned. They may look different from what you planned or thought. But rest assured, God knows what He's doing. Go with it. Step out on faith. Even if you are afraid, follow Him anyway. Trust the process.

Keep me safe, my God, for in you I take refuge. I say to the Lord, "You are my Lord; apart from you I have no good thing." I say to the holy people who are in the land, "They are the noble ones in whom is all my delight." Those who run after other gods will suffer more and more. I will not pour out libations of blood to such gods or take up their names on my lips.

Lord, you alone are my portion and my cup; you make my lot secure. The boundary lines have fallen for me in pleasant places; surely, I have a delightful inheritance. I will praise the Lord, who counsels me; even at night my heart instructs me. I keep my eyes always on the Lord. With him at my right hand, I will not be shaken.

Therefore my heart is glad, and my tongue rejoices; my body also will rest secure, because you will not abandon me to the realm of the dead, nor will you let your faithful one see decay. You make known to me the path of life; you will fill me with joy in your presence, with eternal pleasures at your right hand.

Psalms 16 ~ New International Version

Dear Daddy
(I Can Only Imagine)

Dear Daddy,

I'm writing you this letter to say that although **I have never met you**, I love you. I can only imagine what you were like. **I never saw your face**, but I can only imagine that you were a handsome man standing about 6'2" with pecan-brown, smooth-as-silk skin, beautiful brown eyes, curly black hair, and well-dressed. **I never heard your voice**, but I can only imagine you were soft-spoken, but when you spoke, you spoke with power and authority. When you spoke, everyone listened. **I never felt your touch**, but I can only imagine that it was strong but gentle. I can imagine you holding me tight as you kissed my forehead, telling me how beautiful I was and how much you loved me while stroking my curly black hair (that I got from you) and reassuring me that I would always be safe in your arms. **I never got a chance to smell you**, but I can only imagine that you smelled so good, a scent that only I would remember, a smell of your shirt or your pillow when I held them close to me. Daddy, I just wanted to say although I never met you, I never saw your face, I never heard your voice, I never felt your touch, or I never smelled your scent - I miss you, and I love you. But, in reality, that's all I can do is **IMAGINE!**

Love Your Daughter,

Annette

1/25/18